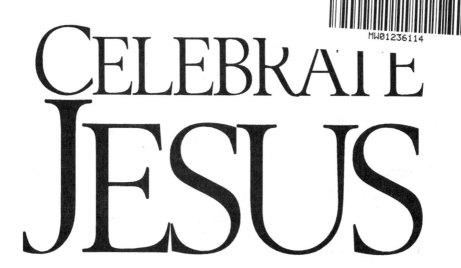

CELEBRATE JESUS

Ten Songs of Testimony and Praise

Arranged by
Marty Hamby

Orchestrations by Marty Hamby, Don Marsh,
Jay Rouse, Richard Kingsmore, Ed Dickinson

Companion Products Available:

Listening Cassette 0-7673-9883-1
(Listening Cassettes available in quantities of ten or more for $3.00 each
from your Music Supplier or Genevox Music Group)

Listening CD 0-7673-9882-3

Accompaniment Cassette 0-7673-9890-4

(Side A Split-track; Side B Instruments only)

Accompaniment CD 0-7673-9889-0 (Split-track only)

Cassette Promo Pak 0-7673-9885-8

CD Promo Pak 0-7673-9887-4

Orchestration 0-7673-9886-6

INSTRUMENTATION: Flute 1-2, Oboe, Clarinet 1-2, Trumpet 1-2-3, French Horn 1-2,
Trombone 1-2-3, Tuba, Percussion, Timpani, Rhythm, Harp, Violin 1-2, Viola, Cello, String Bass,
Alto Sax 1-2 (substitute for French Horn 1-2), Tenor Sax/Baritone Treble Clef (substitute for Trombone 1-2),
Clarinet 3 (substitute for Viola), Bass Clarinet (substitute for Cello), Bassoon (substitute for Cello),
Keyboard String Reduction.

GENEVOX

Code 0-7673-9891-2

CONTENTS

God's people have more reason to celebrate than any other people on earth, for the Christ, who came 2,000 years ago, impacts more than just our calendars. He is the cornerstone of human history – the author and finisher of our faith. In light of the challenges and opportunities of a new century, Christians are being summoned to pray and share Christ through a strategy of prayer, evangelism, and discipleship.

This choral collection is full of variety – and full of Jesus! Marty Hamby has arranged each title to express celebration, adoration, and dedication to the One who stands in the middle of history. Guided by producer Camp Kirkland, Marty has joined his efforts with those of orchestrators Don Marsh, Jay Rouse, Richard Kingsmore, and Ed Dickinson.

Jesus! He stands at the center of it all!

I Will Sing and Bless the Lord

Words and Music by
L. KIRK TALLEY
Arranged by Marty Hamby

6

He has worked a mir-a-cle in me. The unis.

Lord nev-er prom-ised per-fect con-di-tions,

Some-times it would be hard to smile; But the

sing___ and bless the Lord;___ I will lift up His ho - ly name, Hal - le - lu - jah! He has worked a mir - a - cle in me. Oh, hal - le -

Celebrate Jesus (Medley)

with
Celebrate Jesus
Joyful, Joyful, We Adore Thee
All Hail the Power of Jesus' Name

Arranged by Marty Hamby

© Copyright 1998 Van Ness Press, Inc. (ASCAP)
Distributed by GENEVOX (a div. of GMG), Nashville, TN 37234.

15

20

22

To Count for Jesus

Words and Music by
NILES BOROP and LARI GOSS
Arranged by Marty Hamby

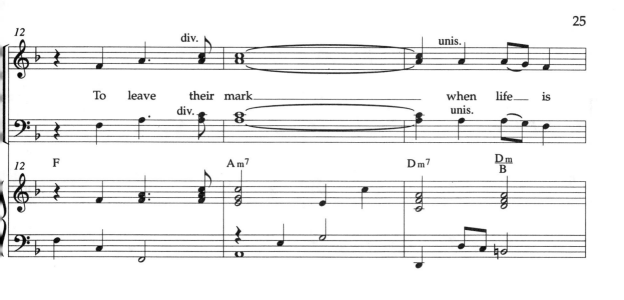

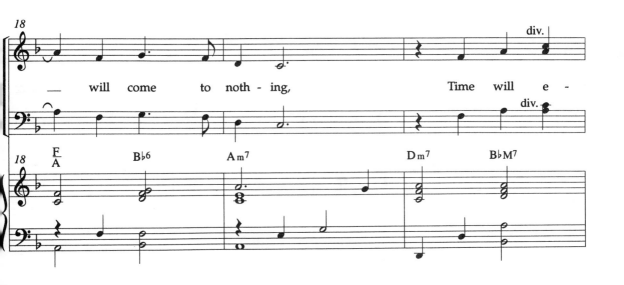

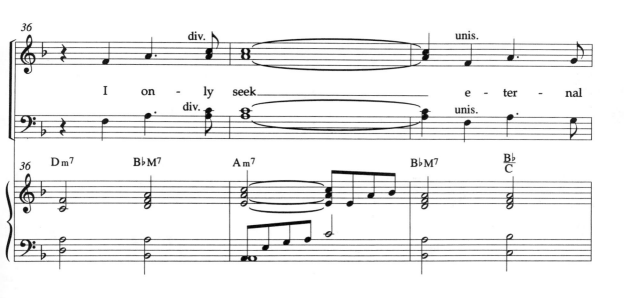

28

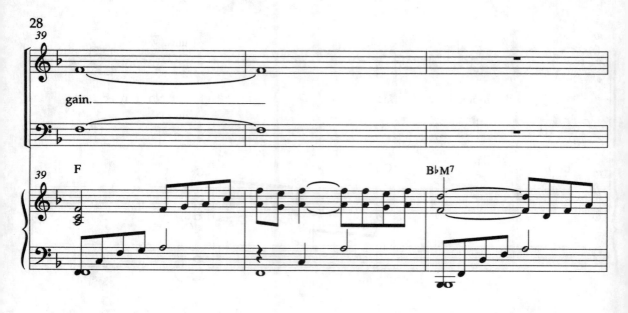

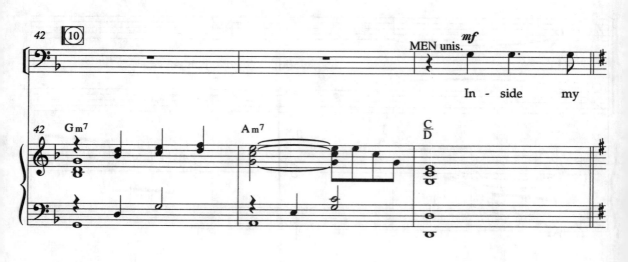

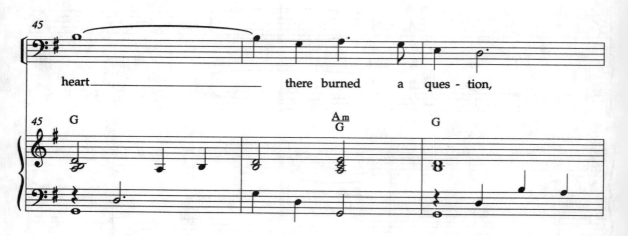

30

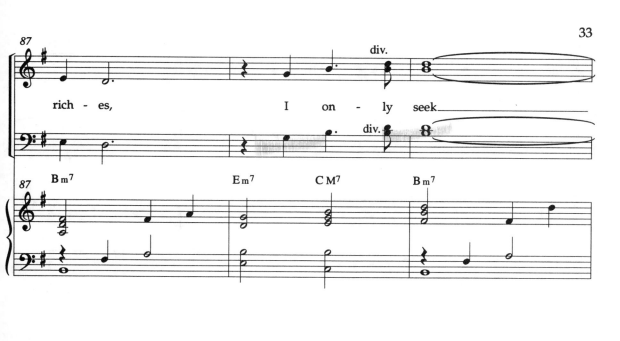

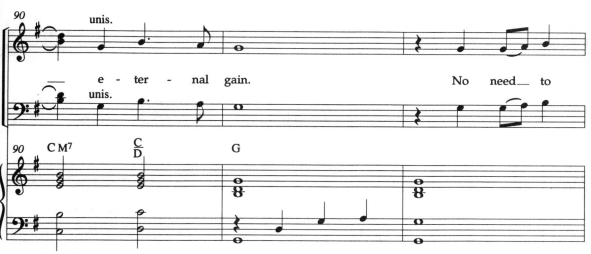

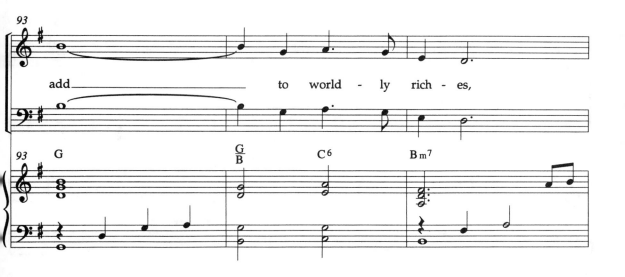

He Never Gave Up On Me

with
Thank You, Lord

Words and Music by
TERRY ROBINSON
Arranged by Marty Hamby

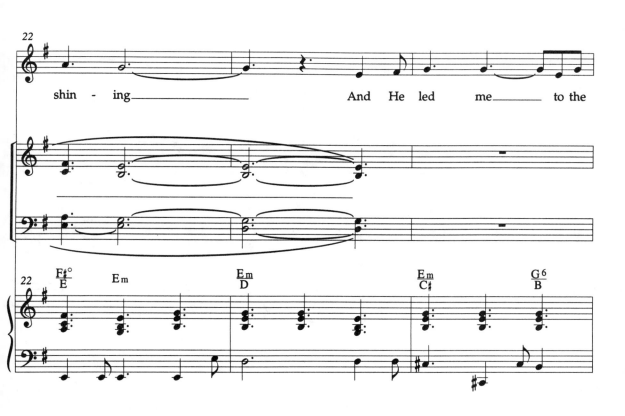

foot of ___ the cross. ___

And

He nev - er gave up on me, ___

And He nev - er gave up on

me.

SOLO

I re - mem - ber when His Spir - it came

42

† "Thank You, Lord" Words and Music by SETH and BESSIE SYKES.

44

46

In Time, On Time, Everytime

Words and Music by
BELINDA LEE SMITH
Arranged by Marty Hamby

50

52

It was un - like - ly then____ to all____ of those men, sure - ly Go - li - ath would fall;____

And when the three He - brew boys____ would - n't

56

fell at Josh - u - a's feet; Ev - 'ry - time

I feel dis - cour - aged, I don't have to

won - der where He'll be, God's been

60

Guide Me, O Thou Great Jehovah

WILLIAM WILLIAMS

JOHN HUGHES
Arranged by Marty Hamby

Open now the crys - tal__ foun - tain

Whence the heal - ing stream doth flow.

Be Thou still my Strength and Shield._____

Be Thou still__ my_____ Strength and Shield.

♩ = ca. 92

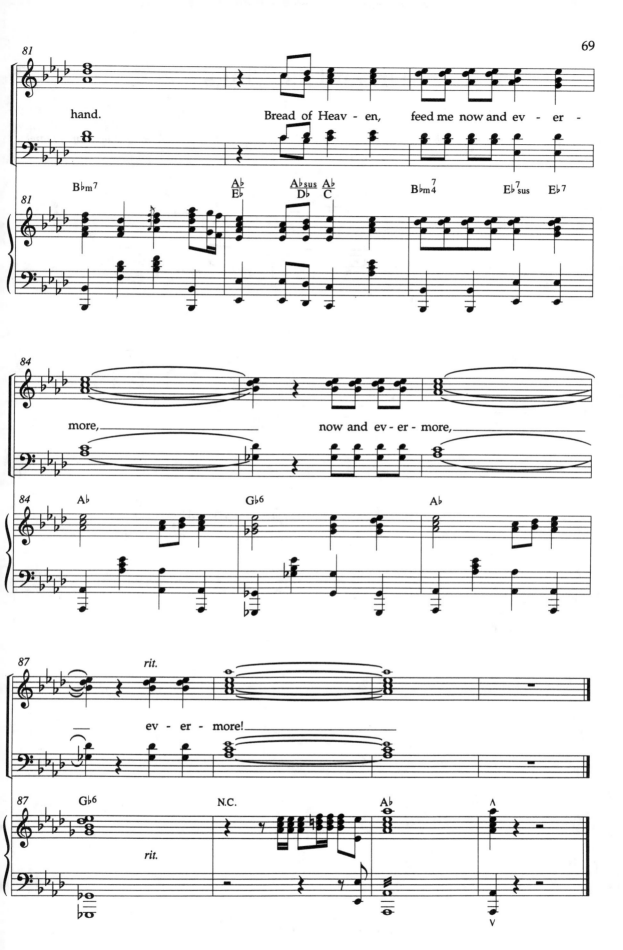

Under His Wings

Words and Music by
WILMA TOMBLIN
Arranged by Marty Hamby

And the en-e-my still looks for me, But what he can't see is that I'm un-der my Lord's wings.

74

76

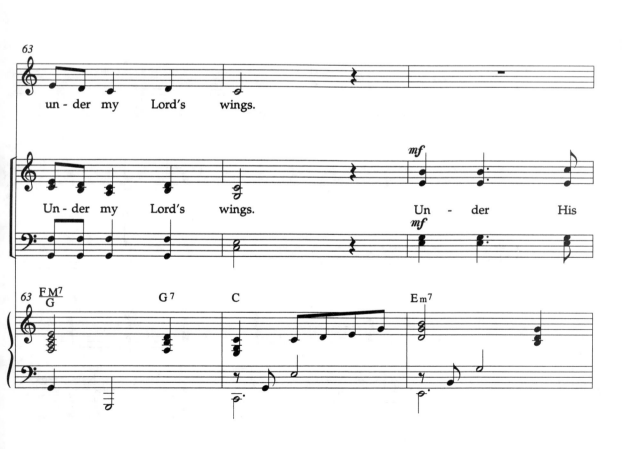

† "Under His Wings" Words by EDGAR P STITES; Music by IRA D. SANKEY.

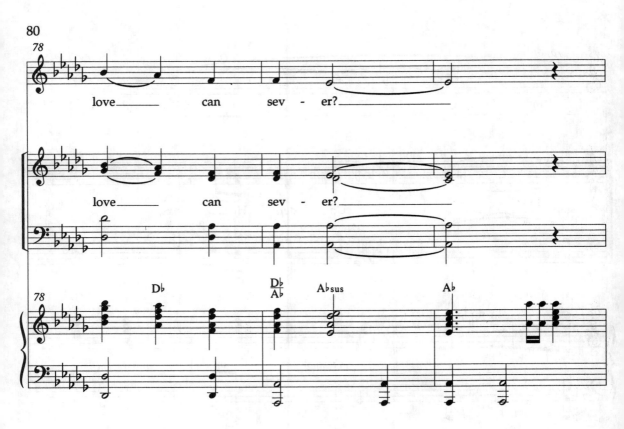

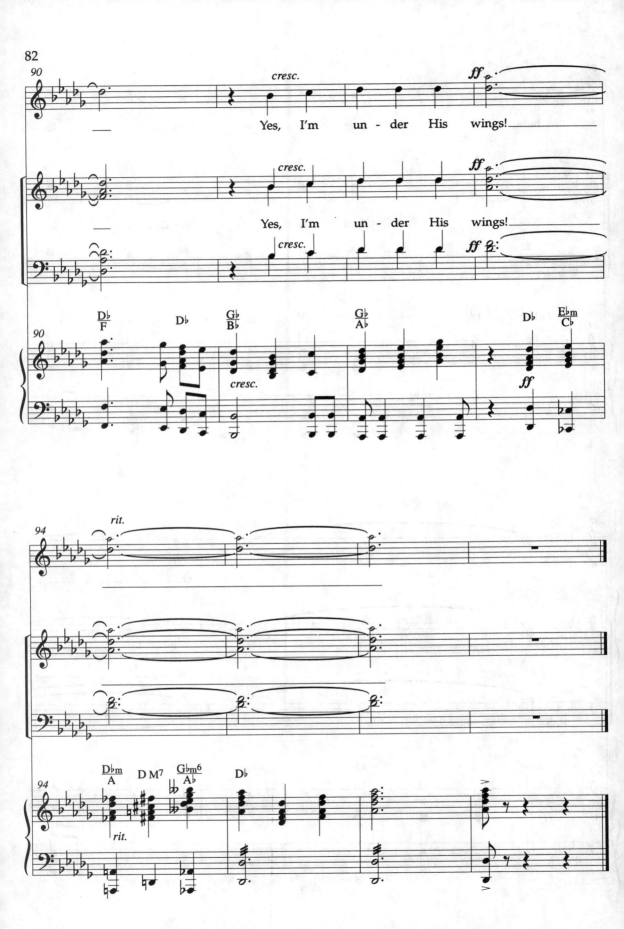

We Ought to Praise Him

Words and Music by
SQUIRE E. PARSONS, JR.
Arranged by Marty Hamby

92

94

Save In the Cross of Jesus

Words and Music by
MIKE HARLAND, LUKE GARRETT
and CHRIS MACHEN
Arranged by Marty Hamby

Congregational Medley

Sing His Name (Medley)

includes
He Keeps Me Singing
Blessed Be the Name
Down at the Cross
Take the Name of Jesus with You

Arranged by Marty Hamby

107

110

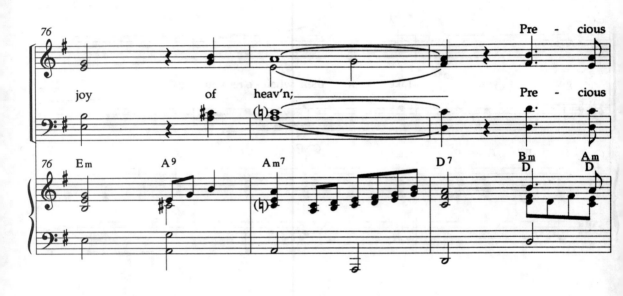

114